Accele

Learn Faster & Improve Your Memory Using the World's Most Advanced Techniques in 12 Hours or Less!

By
Ralph Castle

Ralph Castle

© Copyright 2018 by Ralph Castle - All rights reserved.

The following eBook is reproduced below with the goal of providing information that is as accurate and reliable as possible. Regardless, purchasing this eBook can be seen as consent to the fact that both the publisher and the author of this book are in no way experts on the topics discussed within and that any recommendations or suggestions that are made herein are for entertainment purposes only. Professionals should be consulted as needed prior to undertaking any of the action endorsed herein.

This declaration is deemed fair and valid by both the American Bar Association and the Committee of Publishers Association and is legally binding throughout the United States.

Furthermore, the transmission, duplication or reproduction of any of the following work including specific information will be considered an illegal act irrespective of if it is done electronically or in print. This extends to creating a secondary or tertiary copy of the work or a recorded copy and is only allowed with express written consent from the Publisher. All additional right reserved.

The information in the following pages is broadly considered to be a truthful and accurate account of facts and as such any inattention, use or misuse of the information in question by the reader will render any resulting actions solely under their purview. There are no scenarios in which the publisher or the original author of this work can be in any fashion deemed liable for any hardship or damages that may befall them after undertaking information described herein.

Additionally, the information in the following pages is intended only for informational purposes and should thus be thought of as universal. As befitting its nature, it is presented without assurance regarding its prolonged validity or interim quality. Trademarks that are mentioned are done without written consent and can in no way be considered an endorsement from the trademark holder.

Accelerated Learning

How would you like to increase your reading time even more with this <u>free book</u> on speed reading?

Go Here To Get a **FREE** Digital Copy!

bit.ly/2LeUhlN

Ralph Castle

Contents

Introduction 7
Hour 1: Learning and Memorization Techniques 9
Hour 2: How Good are Your Study Habits Today? 18
Hour 3: Plan of Attack for More Learning Power Overnight..28
Hour 4: Organization—How to Get Twice as Much Done in Half the Time 35
Hour 5: How to Power-Read............................. 42
Hour 6: How to Pre-Read a Lesson—Understand it Before You Read! 51
Hour 7: Note-taking—How to Memorize What You've Read and Put it into Immediate Use.... 54
Hour 8: How to Determine the Chapter's Main Thoughts.. 63
Hour 9: How to Learn by Listening 82
Hour 10: How to Cram before an Exam 88
Hour 11: Social Learning—Remembering Names, Faces, etc. 92
Hour 12: How to Become a Master Reader in Four Easy Steps 97
Conclusion 101

Accelerated Learning

Introduction

Congratulations and thank you for downloading *Accelerated Learning: Learn Faster and Improve Your Memory Using the World's Most Advanced Techniques in 12 Hours or Less!*

The following chapters will discuss how to improve your memory, study smarter, and stay organized when learning a new subject. You will also learn how to power read, take efficient notes, and learn by listening. Many of us were taught incorrectly how to study. As a result, we now lack confidence in our ability to handle new information, but there is good news! Anyone can learn a new subject quickly and easy—they just have to learn how to be efficient learners!

Using the information contained in the pages of this book, anyone can learn a new subject matter in only hours! Whether you are cramming for a college exam, trying to learn a new language, or studying for your first day in a fast-paced new career, this book has you covered! Devote a day to learning and, by tomorrow morning, you'll be ready to face whatever learning challenges you need to overcome. Conquer your fear of studying and jump into a new mindset about your ability to learn fully and quickly!

Your abilities are endless. Get ready to open your mind and expand your horizons!

There are plenty of books on this subject on the market. Thanks again for choosing this one! Every effort was made to ensure it is full of as much useful information as possible, so please enjoy!

Accelerated Learning

Hour 1: Learning and Memorization Techniques

To understand how to better memorize, you must first understand how memory works. Memory is the brain's way of storing information in a symbolic way to help our brains predict future situations and understand those that have passed. As we evolved, we developed the ability to memorize because it was the best way for us to survive.

Our brains are programmed to remember information that is vivid and engaging. It is because of this that many of us have trouble memorizing things that we do not necessarily enjoy learning about. There is a trick to this, though: You must make the information engaging or otherwise fun for you to absorb.

Below, we will discuss some of the best memorization techniques to help your brain absorb and store what you are learning.

Connect & Link: Using this technique, you must create associations between list items and visualize the items to help commit them to memory. For example, let's pretend you are trying to memorize the list of things your boss asked you to do today.

You can create an association cycle. It would look something like this:

- I need to go make the weekly deposit at the bank.
- Because we are depositing Accounts Receivable for the week, Payroll is ready to go out.
- I also need to pass by the accountant's office and pick up paychecks.

- The paychecks will go in the worker's lounge, where we are also out of coffee filters. I will pick up coffee filters on my way back.

Make a Story: This approach works very much like the aforementioned linking method. The difference here is that you don't do the story in a step-by-step manner, but rather in one blanket statement to cover all the necessary information. If we use the same example we used above, this method would look like this:

It's the end of the week, so we are going to deposit our accounts receivable and pay our employees. It is also time to re-stock any supplies we are short on, like coffee filters.

The Location Method: This is a method in which we associate items or terms with specific locations. This one can actually be pretty fun. Let's say you are trying to memorize the names Simon, Jack, and Piggy from *The Lord of the Flies*. You can imagine you are on a deserted island. Imagine you are walking in the sand and you see some children playing Simon Says. Further up the shore, someone is carving a jack-o-lantern, and then a pig runs by. Simple? Yes, but also very efficient. Many master memorizers use this method, and it has been a popular memorization method since the early Romans.

Draw a Mind Map: This involves visualizing a map that will direct you from one point of information to the next. We remember pictures better than we remember words. You can even draw out the map on paper and memorize the image that way.

Use the Peg System: Have you ever noticed that pin numbers, lock combinations, and phone digits are easier to memorize—sometimes—than names? There's a reason for that, and it can lend itself to power-memorizing in a method called the Peg System. If you need to memorize a certain set of information in a particular order, this is the best system for it.

First, you memorize the words alongside with an easy to associate number. That will go something like this:

You need to memorize the names of the sisters from *Little Women* in order of age from oldest to youngest.

Meg - Meg rhymes with egg and eggs come by the dozen. You'll associate her with the number 12.
Jo - Jo rhymes with "no," which is 0.
Beth - Beth is the only name with four letters. She gets assigned 4.
Amy - Amy starts with the same sound as 8, which is her number assignment.

Now you don't need to memorize their names in that order. You only need to memorize 12-0-4-8.

Visit the Roman Room: This technique incorporates a little bit of all the previous techniques. When used correctly, this is an amazing method for memorization that can be nothing short of life-changing.

Try remembering these words in order:

Poster, Ankle, Television, Lamp, Microwave, Atom, Marker, Tornado, Headphones, Hamster

These words have no associations between them so they will be difficult to remember if you don't implement a technique.

The Roman Room provides a technique for memorizing items that have no link to one another. Think of a square room you are familiar with—your bedroom or your office, perhaps. As you walk into that room, imagine this:

Walking into that room, look at the nearest corner to your left shoulder. That will be number 1. The next wall, moving clockwise, is number 2. The corner next to that is number 3,

Accelerated Learning

and so on until all the walls and corners are numbered.

If done correctly, you'll have corner 5 opposite corner 1 and wall 2 opposite of wall 6. There will be eight numbers in all so far. Assign number 9 to the floor and 10 to the ceiling.

The more you use this method, the easier it will be to recall these locations by number. To help yourself memorize, you can practice writing and labeling the parts of the room in a list. Write 1–10 on a piece of paper.

Next, we will place the items throughout the room, going clockwise from the door, in the order in which they would appear. To remember the items in our earlier list, we might do this:

```
3        4         5


2    9  10        6


1        8         7
         DOOR
```

The poster on the back of the door is facing number 1. To see it, we can slide our ankle against position 2 and close the door. Then we will walk over and turn on the television, then the lamp, and put our food in the microwave. We continue with this pattern throughout the house so that everything makes sense in the order of the list. Incorporate the items in the order you need to remember them, and then use all your senses to make them a part of the scene.

SEA is a common reference you might hear in memorization. It means Senses, Emotions, Actions. You incorporate these three things into organizing your memories.

Hour 2: How Good are Your Study Habits Today?

What's your study style? Does it work? Do you even know?

Most people don't. The biggest obstacle to learning new things is that to expand our knowledge, we must first have knowledge of how to make the best use of our study time. This is a struggle for a lot of people of all different ages and backgrounds.

Statistically, three out of four students don't study as much as they should, yet three out of four students also say that they feel their study system is adequate. Why is that? It's simple—most of them never learned how to study in the first place.

What about you? Have you ever wondered if your own study system is a bust?

Below, you will find an exam that can help you determine just that. Take your time on the questions and answer honestly, and then read on to see what your answers mean about your current learning abilities.

Self-Assessment in Study Practices

Read and consider each of the statements below, then place an X in the column that has the most appropriate answer.

Reading Text Books	**Rarely**	**Some**	**Often**
I look for a main idea in the text.			
I make sure I find definitions of new words.			
I keep track of questions I have as I read.			

I skim headings, charts, questions, and photos before I read.			
I apply the reading to familiar concepts and build from what I already know.			

Taking Notes	Rarely	Some	Often
I keep track of notes on materials as I read them.			
I make sure to take notes during class lectures and presentations.			
I reorganize my notes after I take them, so they are neater in appearance. I might even type them.			
I compare my notes with those of friends and classmates to ensure I didn't miss			

Accelerated Learning

key points and understood appropriately.			
I try to organize my notes into organized and meaningful sets of ideas and details.			

Studying	Rarely	Some	Often
I seek out a quiet place for studying where I know I will not be distracted.			
I don't cram. I study for a pre-determined set of time and then take a break before studying again.			
I make sure all my necessary study tools are available to me before I sit down to work.			

I set goals for myself during each study session.			
I study for at least two hours outside of class per hour in class each week.			

Memorizing	Rarely	Some	Often
I study when I am feeling most energetic, so I know I will not be too tired to concentrate.			
I quiz myself to make sure I know all the information I need to gain from the materials.			
If I am having a difficult time understanding my reading, I will read it out loud so I can hear it.			

I use my own words when I write my notes.			
I create associations in my mind to help me memorize.			

Preparing for Tests	**Rarely**	**Some**	**Often**
Whenever possible, I find classmates or friends to study with.			
I predict the key elements of my lessons to give myself an idea of what will be most important to know on a test.			
I seek help from someone whenever I don't understand something.			
I take an inventory of the elements I already know and the ones I still need to work on			

before I sit down to study for an exam.			
I do all my homework and study sessions at the required and scheduled times.			

Managing Your Time	**Rarely**	**Some**	**Often**
I start papers and projects as soon as they are assigned to me.			
I keep a to-do list to remind me of things that I might otherwise forget.			
I maintain a planner to keep track of personal and academic activities.			
I begin studying for exams several days before they are scheduled.			

I keep my schedule balanced to allow enough time for school, work, and personal functions, including making sure I have time to have fun.			

Now that you have completed the self-assessment, you will need to determine your score. Points are as follows:

Rarely = 0   **Some = 5**   **Often = 10**

There are thirty questions in this test. Use the scoring system below to figure out your overall score.

Answers of *Rarely*: _____ x 0 = _____

Answers of *Some*: _____ x 5 = _____

Answers of *Often*: _____ x 10

= _____

Total

=
_____
_____
___

Here's what your score means:

A total score of 35–50 means your study skills seem to be well established.

A total score of less than 35 means you need to figure out a better system.

If you did not score well, don't worry. Study skills are not well taught to us when we are young. As a result, many people encounter lifelong obstacles in learning. You are not alone.

Thankfully, continuing this book can help you advance your learning potential.

If you did score well, great job! Keep on reading to discover ways to make your study system reap even greater rewards for you in the process of lifelong education!

Nothing in this world can take the place of persistence.
Talent will not: nothing is more common than unsuccessful men with talent.
Genius will not: unrewarded genius is almost a proverb.
Education will not: the world is full of educated derelicts.
Persistence and determination alone are omnipotent.
-Calvin Coolidge

Hour 3: Plan of Attack for More Learning Power Overnight

"Who needs sleep?" This is often the mantra of a college student or otherwise busy person. Of course, the joke is that most people don't have time for sleep between work and learning, and sometimes balancing a family, not to mention your personal time, which—face it—everyone needs!

Did you know, though, that you can actually learn while you sleep? Your brain never stops working. Studies have actually shown evidence that the moments we are asleep are when our brain works its hardest to file away the information we gathered throughout the preceding day. Wouldn't it be great if we could harness those efforts and learn the things we want to learn?

Accelerated Learning

Guess what? You absolutely can!

Many speed-learners have discovered that they can actually take charge of how their brain functions during sleep, allowing them to use their snooze time as bonus study time.

A recent study by German scientists proved this method to be valid when they had a whole group of subjects learn to speak Dutch as they slept.

The experiment was actually brilliantly simple. They assembled their test subjects, then split them into three groups. One group listened to a Dutch language instructional audio as they slept. Another as they were awake, but busy doing other things. The third group listened to and studied the tape during their waking hours.

Amazingly, the subjects who listened to the tape as they slept seemed to learn at a quicker and easier pace than both other test subject groups.

What does this mean?

You can learn a foreign language while you sleep.

Plan to listen to a calming instructional audio of foreign language instruction as you fall asleep and throughout the night. You'll find that you're picking up words in no time!

In another study conducted in 2013, sixty healthy adults were asked to use a computer program for a new memory test. They used the program to put a virtual object in a certain location on the screen. Upon placing the item in the location, they would hear a specialized tune.

After placing the items in the chosen locations, they took a 90-minute nap. During this nap, they slept with no sounds playing. They got up, were asked if they heard any music as they slept. Some dreamed about the music, but none heard it for sure. When asked where the items had been placed, none seemed to remember. They then did some regular daytime activities, then returned to the program and placed the items again, hearing the tune with each placement. Then, they took a second 90-minute nap. During that nap, the placement tune from the computer program was played multiple times. Upon waking, none of the test subjects remembered hearing the tune, but many of them did remember where the items had been placed.

Queuing your mind with sounds has proven to be a great way to memorize information as you sleep.

Building on that, researchers did another sound-based sleep study. This time, they taught various guitar melodies to a group of people using the well-known video game, *Guitar Hero*. Afterward, the subjects were told to take a nap and were then asked to play the songs again.

Some could remember the melody. Others could not. The difference between the two groups? Those that remembered how to play the melody had been listening to it as they slept. The others had slept in silence.

Playing back a new song you've learned can help you memorize how to play it on your favorite instrument.

In further studies, it was proven that we can actually learn to lock away our memories and protect them as we sleep, also. This is because our brains use a sort of tagging system to separate important memories from those that aren't. Have you ever wondered why you can remember the name of your first-grade teacher, but not the name of the customer you helped at work yesterday?

As a child, it was important to know your teacher's name, so your brain made sure to file it. In the current world, you help so many customers in a day that they all become a blur to you. Your brain files them in a drawer labeled "unnecessary information."

There's a way to take control of this, though. If we link sounds with memories, even unimportant ones, we can hold onto them better.

Clapping the syllables of an important piece of information, or turning that information into a melody in our minds can help us bring back the information we need at a later date. If we set a particular set of information to a popular tune and listen to that tune as we sleep, when our brains are busy filing, we will wake up remembering the information.

Our brain activity gets slower at night during certain phases of sleep. Slow Wave Sleep or SWS is the part of your sleep routine in which our short-term memories get moved to our long-term storage. If we are listening to a tune that recalls that short-term memory as we sleep, then that memory is in front of the line when filing time comes. Rather than being dumped as unnecessary, it gets pushed into the "must remember" column of our minds.

If you want to learn while you sleep, the best way to do it is to set up a system of sounds that will help you remember, then get good sleep (so you don't skip any important phases) as those sounds are played.

This is how spelling bee champions, medical students, and competitive memory learners do some of their best studying. It can help you, too!

Who needs sleep? You do, silly! But you can use it to your advantage with a little bit of forethought and planning.

Sweet dreams!

Accelerated Learning

Hour 4: Organization—

How to Get Twice as Much Done in Half the Time

Don't say you don't have enough time. You have exactly the same number of hours per day that was given to Helen Keller, Pasteur, Michelangelo, Mother Teresa, Leonardo da Vinci, Thomas Jefferson, and Albert Einstein. ~Life's Little Instruction Book, compiled by H. Jackson Brown, Jr.

Do you ever feel like you're just spinning your wheels and getting nowhere? Have you ever sat for a full day, been busy, then at the end of the day looked around and realized you didn't accomplish much?

We've all been there. A lack of feeling productive can be a hard blow to anyone, particularly someone who is trying their hardest to absorb and implement new learning in their life. We are all trying to do the most we can with the least amount of time possible. We chase the thrill of hitting the checkbox on our to-do list, but we all know that the to-do list is never-ending. As soon as you check off three things, you've got five more staring you in the face.

It's a frustrating cycle.

The first step of feeling more productive is learning to redefine what productivity means to you. You should never base the worth of a day put in at work on the mere number of items you managed to cross off your list. After all, one task might take all day, while six others can be done in an hour.

You have to learn to value the quality of your work ahead of the quantity. Productivity is knocking down the most important chores of each day. If you have time to tackle smaller ones, great. If not, don't worry—they will eventually grow into important tasks in their own time. Get what needs done finished now and let everything else wait its turn.

In other words, prioritize! Some find it easier to prioritize tasks if they take inventory of the benefits they will reap from finishing each task. Whether your goal is to close a deal at work or get the bathroom cleaned, you need to visualize how great it will feel when you're finished. Don't focus on the chore ahead, but on how great things will be when the task is over!

Of course, you have to do this rationally. You might think you'll feel better tonight if you call in and clean the house and bake yourself a cake, but are you going to enjoy that cake when you're out a job? If the answer is no, you need to make another plan.

Once you've decided what your main priority is, you'll need to set yourself a timeline. A task will take as long to finish as what we allow ourselves to do it. If you say, "I'll get to it sometime this week," you're less likely to successfully accomplish the task on time than if you tell yourself you'll get it done a day early.

Your deadline should always be well before the panic threshold.

If you promise your boss he will have a report by next Monday, tell yourself you'll get it to him Friday. If you know you need the house cleaned for guests by Saturday, work on it Wednesday night. See the theme? Not only will this take a lot of stress out of your life, but it will also improve your reputation at work. You'll become someone that people know they can depend on, which will make you an asset to your company.

The same rules can apply when it comes to studying. You know midterms are coming up? Start studying now. Don't wait until the weekend before or you're going to find yourself in a sticky situation.

Accelerated Learning

You should also familiarize yourself with "Burst Work." Burst Work is a simple concept.

If we move too slowly with a project, we will get bored. If we move too quickly, we will get fatigued. Take frequent breaks and refocus, then get back to work. Move around. Dance to your favorite song. Walk the dog. Pick up all of your study materials and move to a different spot.

When you change it up and take a moment to yourself, it's so much easier to turn the page to the next set of notes. You'll memorize more of what you're learning, too, since your brain won't be tuning out from overflow.

You can also physically change the way you are working. Sitting at a desk all day can seem suffocating and crippling. Move your workstation somewhere else. If possible, move to a standing desk. Your blood flow will increase and recharge your brain. When you get tired of moving around or standing, make yourself comfortable somewhere else—just not too comfortable. If you get sleepy, you're doing it wrong.

You might also find it helpful to make yourself a list. If you prioritize your tasks and list them in the order you need to get them done in, you'll be able to visualize your day and the process you'll need to take to get to your goal.

Tasks that are pressing should come first, no matter how much you don't want to do them. If you're looking forward to an easier subject of study or one that interests you more, you might benefit from putting it at the end. You can treat a chore as a reward! There's no rule saying you can't.

By practicing a little bit of discipline in your study or work, you can find a routine that works for you and completes everything on time and with minimal stress. Structure your day to accomplish these goals and schedule breaks and a reward. You'll get a lot more accomplished and feel like you've put in half the effort.

Hour 5: How to Power-Read

Think about how much quicker you could learn if you were able to speed up your reading by 30 percent. Wouldn't that save you a ton of time?

A lot of people have found that increased reading is very doable for them. Increasing reading speed is achieved by learning to control your fine motor movement.

When used properly, there is a no-fail method of gaining this skill. Below, we will outline the process in its entirety.

First, though, you'll need to understand several definitions and abilities that are specific to speed-reading and its process.

Fixation Minimization: This is minimizing the length and number of fixations that happen in each line to increase your reading speed. In other words, you don't read at a constant speed, but you, instead, make a sequence of jumps throughout the lines of the document. Each ends with a fixation of your focus area—this is a sort of temporary snapshot of the text you're looking at. These fixations typically last between a quarter and a half of a second to those who aren't trained in speed reading.

If you want to demonstrate a fixation to yourself, close one eye and put the tip of your finger on that eyelid. Slowly scan across a straight horizontal line with your other eye. Every distinct movement you feel through your eyelid is a period of fixation.

Eliminate Regression: A person untrained in speed reading engages in regression and back-reading throughout about thirty percent of their total reading time. Regression is a conscious rereading of material, while back-reading is the inadvertent skipping back because of misplacement of fixation. If you can stop falling into these traps, you'll have already increased your reading speed significantly.

Increase your Horizontal Peripheral Vision: Most of us use central focus when we read, but not our horizontal peripheral vision. This cuts out fifty percent or four possible words per fixation. We can read twice as fast by learning to focus horizontally on the page, rather than just centrally.

So how do we do these things?

They come with practice and honing the skill, but there is a technique that seems to work well when applied correctly.

The Technique

To make speed reading work, you need to do three things:

Accelerated Learning

1. Learn the technique fully. Study it and understand completely what is required of you to succeed.
2. Learn to apply this technique by conditioning. This means practice, practice, practice.
3. Learn to test yourself for both speed and comprehension. One is useless without the other.

Remember, these are three different skillsets. You cannot be successful unless you focus on them as separate entities of a "team" of skills to achieve the major goal of faster reading.

As a rule, most speed readers practice the technique at a speed that is three times what their ultimate target speed is. Therefore, if you currently read 300 words per minute and you want to learn to read 900 words per minute, you'll have to practice for 2,700 words per minute. That's six pages in one minute and ten seconds per page.

Seem impossible? It's not.

The first step is determining your baseline. To do this, find a book that lays flat on a table. Count the number of words there are in five lines. Divide this by five. This is the average number of words per line in that section.

Next, count the number of lines there are in five pages. Divide this by five to figure out the average number of lines per page. Multiply the two averages together. The result is the average number of words per page. This is the first piece of information you need in discovering your current read-speed.

Now, set a timer for one minute, mark your starting spot, and begin reading. Don't read faster or slower than normal. Read at a level where you are comprehending the text. After the timer goes off, mark your stopping point.

Multiply your average words per line by the number of lines. This is your words per minute.

Next, you'll need to figure out your trackers and pacers. You can minimize the duration of your fixations, as well as regression and back-skipping by using trackers and pacers. When you were counting the number of words or lines earlier, did you use your finger or a pen? If you did, you used a tracker. When you use a visual aid to guide your fixation, you improve accuracy and efficiency. It can keep you from losing your place, and it can keep your mind focused on exactly where your eyes need to be.

You don't need to write in your book with a pen. Just trace each line with the pen with the cap on. Even visualizing the drawing of the line will help your eyes and mind stay focused. Also, your eyes will automatically want to follow the pen. This will help you pick up the pace as you read.

Now, take the opportunity to practice this. Track and pace using a pen. Underline the lines of the book as you go through them, focusing on the tip of the cap. You don't need to comprehend what you're reading right now. That will come later. Right now, you are focusing on speed. Challenge yourself to read each line in one second, speeding up as you go through the pages.

Once you are comfortable reading a line in half a second, you're ready to move on to the next practice set.

Reread the page. As you do, let the words process imagery in your mind, but do not decrease your speed. When you reach the end, think back on what you just read. Did you understand it? If not, practice again, but at a different place in the book. Keep going until you finish with understanding. **Teaching yourself not to daydream is half the battle with**

this skill. In the end, you should be able to comprehend what you have read.

Next, you will need to work on **Perceptual Expansion.** You will still notice notifications or popups at other parts of the screen of your phone or computer, even if you are focusing on the center, won't you? This is the same concept we want to bring into your reading.

Peripheral vision can be trained to register more of the page to increase your reading speed by up to 300%! Around fifty percent of your current reading time is spent reading margins of the page that have no content.

You can also increase your reading by cutting out words. For example, read the sentence "Every month, on the first Tuesday, Joanne goes to get her hair cut in town."

Now, reread it and cut out the first and last two words of the sentence.

"On the first Tuesday, Joanne goes to get her hair cut"

The meaning of the statement is the same. We can guess she is getting it cut on the first Tuesday of the month and that she has to cut her hair in town. Most sentences work this way. Focus on the meatier part of the sentences, and you can read them faster.

After practicing all these skills, you can recalculate your Words per Minute the same way you did in the beginning.

One final tip: When studying, don't read two assignments instead of just one just because you can read twice as fast. Read the assignment twice instead. Two read-throughs mean twice the studying without confusing yourself with text from multiple sources in the same study session.
Good luck!

Accelerated Learning

Hour 6: How to Pre-Read a Lesson—Understand it Before You Read!

It is counterproductive to invest too much time in pre-reading a chapter, but there are benefits if you do it wisely.

The first step in successfully pre-reading is to look ahead at chapter titles and subtitles. What is the chapter going to be about? What are the key themes that the chapter will focus on? This will help you determine what parts of the reading are most important. You can even formulate questions ahead of time and keep an eye out for the answers you know you will need.

By the same token, many textbooks feature questions throughout the chapters. Often, these will be at the end of chapter sections. Take a look at those for ideas of what you are supposed to be learning.

You should also read the chapter introductions. If there is no official chapter introduction, read the first paragraph of the chapter. This is the lead-in to the lesson and will give you a great idea of what to expect in the further text. Once you move past that, go into the bold subheadings and read the first sentence of the first paragraph of those subsequent sections. If the first sentence does not contain information but is instead used as a means to catch your attention, you'll want to skip to the second sentence.

Also make sure you check out the photographs, graphs, and other visual aids that accompany the paragraph. Read captions and understand what they are telling you with these visual aids.

Also, skim the chapter for any terms and definitions that will be important to you in your

Accelerated Learning

reading. These are usually italicized or bold text. Finally, read the chapter summary.

Once you have pre-read the chapter, you are ready to go back to the beginning and read it in its entirety. You will be amazed at how much more you gain from reading the chapter after pre-reading to start!

Hour 7: Note-taking—How to Memorize What You've Read and Put it into Immediate Use

Some of the biggest struggles we have with studying involve note-taking. Often, when listening to a lecture or reading a chapter, we allow the process of taking notes to overwhelm us. We are in such a hurry to write down the information that we feel will be most pertinent that we struggle to organize them into a study guide that will make sense to us later. At the same time, we are only half-listening because we are too busy writing to make sense of what we hear.

This is why the process of Active Learning is so crucial in taking notes. This means that, when you are taking the notes, you need to not only be hearing, but you also need to be understanding and organizing the information you are hearing. It is less important to write down everything than it is to make sure your notes will make sense when you go back to read them. Effective note-taking requires presence of thought and effort and a commitment to review the notes at later times.

The simple act of taking notes, if done correctly, can be beneficial in memorizing facts, but you can't rely on the act of writing the information down alone. We learn best when we review the information at least once, but preferably a couple times or more. This is why it's so important to be able to go back and see what you wrote in an organized matter that makes sense to you, even when the lecture is long over.

Note-taking is a four-stage process:

1. **Note-taking**

a. This part of the process works best if you prepare a page ahead of time to ensure your notes are organized cohesively and repetitively. Most like to pose an essential question at the beginning of their notes to focus their mind on key learning objectives and discussion points.

b. It's also helpful to separate your page into two columns. The first column should take up a third of the page to the left. This column should be left blank at first, and all notes should be taken and transcribed into the larger, right-hand column. Then, when other questions or information come up, the space on the left can be used to insert pertinent information where it belongs.

c. You should always take notes in your own words. Write the information in the same way you would repeat it back to a classmate or friend if asked. If you write your notes word-for-word, you risk not understanding the material when you read back through it later. This also challenges you to understand the information as you are taking the notes instead of just writing what you hear.

d. Leave plenty of room in your notes to add in information later as it comes up.

e. It is helpful to devise and put to use a personal set of abbreviations and symbols that will save you time when note-taking. Make sure this system is consistent throughout your notes and is something you will understand when you go back to review.

f. Whenever possible, write the information in a short phrase instead of a long sentence.

g. Use lists and bullet points, if possible, to minimize time and space.

h. Listen for hints from the lecturer or source. "This is important," "This will be on the test," or "Make sure you remember," are all hints that the information being shared should be put in your notes.

i. It's okay not to take note of things you already know and are confident about.

j. When you review, use a highlighter to keep track of the places you are struggling with, so you can review them specifically. Use a separate color highlighter to mark places in your notes that are unclear so you can ask someone else or do research to determine what you have missed.

2. Note-Making

a. Review and revise the content of your notes.
b. Write questions into your notes to fill in gaps in your understanding.
c. Use labels to connect parts of your notes to other relevant sections.
d. If possible, compare notes with a classmate to make sure you understood the material and didn't miss any key factors in the lecture.

3. **Note Interaction**
   a. Make time to write a short summary that incorporates the essential subject of the lecture and answers any potential questions you have. Use your notes as a point of reference. Keep this summary and re-read it to study.
   b. Using your highlighted sections, review your notes from the most difficult aspects to the easiest.

c. Schedule time each day to review your notes.

4. **Note Reflection**
   a. If you can, exchange notes with a classmate and write feedback for one another on the competency of the notes that have been taken.
   b. Leading up to tests and exams, make sure you review your notes often and quiz yourself on their content. This will help you memorize important information. Answers should come to you easily without having to sift through a cloud of information when test day arrives.

To help with the process, there are some other tips that can also be considered.

- **Rest well.** Even the most organized note-takers suffer when it comes to notating lectures and lessons if they have not slept. When we are tired, our minds don't work correctly. We can't pay attention, and we wind up missing key parts of the lecture because we tune out or stay focused on unimportant information. When our brains have had an adequate sleep, they work better. They focus harder, and they absorb and sort the information in a way that is helpful to us.

- **Take care of your health.** This means that you should stay hydrated and eat a balanced diet. Your brain shrinks and gets confused when it isn't hydrated. You also have a harder time focusing if you are hungry or bogged down by high sugar or other unhealthy food choices. Make your brain happy by feeding it well and making sure it is properly hydrated. It will reward you.

- **Exercise your brain.** Your brain is often treated as if it is solely used for cognitive or emotional purposes, but it is the control center of your entire body. The more you exercise your brain, the healthier your entire body gets. This includes the brain. You'll also want to give yourself time for quiet meditation whenever possible. This helps your brain find focus when necessary.

Challenge: Once you have mastered the note-taking and memorization skill set, you are ready to move forward on your path to better and faster learning. Take a moment to practice some of these techniques, then—when you're ready—move forward with a notebook in hand and a pen at the ready to try out your new note-taking skills on the next chapter of this book.

Hour 8: How to Determine the Chapter's Main Thoughts

Isn't it frustrating when we are told to determine the main thought of a reading only to start reading and not be able to make a clear determination of what that main thought should be? Sometimes, it seems like the thoughts of a particular text are scattered all over the place without any cohesive process involved.

What's worse—when a student goes to highlight their notes or a selection of text to determine important information, they sometimes look back to find they've highlighted the majority of what they have reviewed. How can that be helpful? In short, it isn't.

Determining the main idea or theme of a reading is absolutely necessary for adequate and effective studying. Fortunately, there are ways you can do this.

1. Find the main idea of individual paragraphs. Not everything in a paragraph matters. Usually, the most important piece of information found in a paragraph is the first sentence or topic sentence. Sometimes, it will be the last sentence in the paragraph, though, and that can also be confusing. Even worse, the main idea is sometimes left unstated entirely, and you have to figure out for yourself what the paragraph is trying to tell you. Below, we will outline some examples for you to review and learn from:

Source Paragraph	Idea
I don't wish to deny that the flattened, minuscule head of the large-bodied Stegosaurus houses little	**Dinosaur intelligence can't be determined based on the size**

brain from our subjective, top-heavy perspective, but I do wish to assert that we should not expect more of the beast. First of all, large animals have relatively smaller brains than related, small animals. The correlation of brain size with body size among kindred animals (all reptiles, all mammals, for example) is remarkably regular. As we move from small to large animals, from mice to elephants or small lizards to Komodo dragons, brain size increases, but not as fast as body size. In other words, bodies grow faster	**of their brains alone.** The author doesn't come outright and state that this is his main idea anywhere in the paragraph, but we can definitely tell what he is getting at based on the way he words his thoughts.

than brains, and large animals have low ratios of brain weight to body weight. In fact, brains grow only about two-thirds as fast as bodies. Since we have no reason to believe that large animals are consistently stupider than their smaller relatives, we must conclude that large animals require relatively less brain to do as well as smaller animals. If we do not recognize this relationship, we are likely to underestimate the mental power of very large animals, dinosaurs in particular.

-Stephen Jay Gould, "Were Dinosaurs Dumb?"	
SCIENTISTS HAVE LEARNED TO SUPPLEMENT THE SENSE OF SIGHT IN NUMEROUS WAYS. In front of the tiny pupil of the eye they put, on Mount Palomar, a great monocle 200 inches in diameter, and with it see 2000 times farther into the depths of space. Or they look through a small pair of lenses arranged as a microscope into a drop of water or blood and magnify by as much as 2000 diameters the	**Scientists have made great strides in assisting with vision impairment.**

living creatures there, many of which are among man's most dangerous enemies. Or, if we want to see distant happenings on earth, they use some of the previously wasted electromagnetic waves to carry television images which they re-create as light by whipping tiny crystals on a screen with electrons in a vacuum. Or they can bring happenings of long ago and far away as colored motion pictures, by arranging silver atoms and color-absorbing molecules to force light waves into the patterns of original

This paragraph has a very clear topic and conclusion sentence, both of which have been capitalized as examples. These help keep the focus on the main idea without having to think too much of the information.

reality. Or if we want to see into the center of a steel casting or the chest of an injured child, they send the information on a beam of penetrating short-wave X rays, and then convert it back into images we can see on a screen or photograph.
THUS ALMOST EVERY TYPE OF ELECTROMAGNETIC RADIATION YET DISCOVERED HAS BEEN USED TO EXTEND OUR SENSE OF SIGHT IN SOME WAY.

George Harrison, *"Faith and the Scientist"*

2. You can also find the theme of a text by determining the section ideas. A section is when a text divides a chapter into smaller subgroups. Usually, each of these groups will be given its own heading, aside from just the paragraph title. It is possible to use these headings to determine the idea of what the major theme of the section will likely be. In the following examples, you will see how each of these ideas will relate to the heading of the section and what that should tell you about key points to look for during your reading.

Source Heading	Idea
Providing Nesting Sites Found in the book *"Beginner Beekeeping"* under *Chapter Three: Pollinator Conservation*	The focus of this section will clearly be in providing suitable nesting for the bees you intend to keep. You should look for similarities and

	differences in how nesting should be set up regarding geographic location as well as precautionary warnings and hints for better nesting.
Application of Proportions Found in the book *"University Level Pre-Algebra"* under *Chapter 5: Ratio & Proportion*	This section will work teach you how to use proportions in future math problems. You should look for the definition of proportions as well as how they relate to ratios. Also look for keywords that might be a hint that proportions are needed in word problems.

3. All sections of the book should eventually relate back to the main focus of the chapter, itself. Every section will be

related to the chapter title. Don't forget this when you are looking for the main idea. Sometimes, you can be led astray by a section title because you have forgotten that it relates to a larger theme. The same is true for focusing too hard on chapter titles and not the title of the book as a whole.

Always use the main theme of the textbook as a key structure in your note-taking. Examples are included below.

Source Title	Idea
Film Editing: Theory and Practice	Chapters contained in this book focus on things like computer software, the structure of film, and how to cut scenes in a way that does not distract the viewer. A section titled "Movie-making software" could easily lead a reader astray. They

	might get lost in the technical structure of the software, itself, and forget that they are learning how to edit a film. This is one way that it is important to always relate your reading back to the main focus.
Forming a Nation	This textbook is clearly about the cultural, legal, and historical requirements of building an independent government. In the cultural chapters, it could be easy to get lost in the text and forget that the goal of the chapters is to discuss how a nation is formed and not just to outline religious or lifestyle differences throughout the world.

4. The wisest way to keep track of your reading in a way that will make sense to you is to write your note outline as you read, especially if the reading is particularly dense. You can use your notebook to rewrite difficult-to-understand parts of the reading in a way that will make better sense to you later when you do your review. Make sure that you limit your writing, so you aren't just copying the text (a sentence per paragraph is a good rule of thumb). You can also use an outline style or bullet-based set up to make your written notes easier to navigate. Below, you will find some examples.

Source Paragraph	Note Example
"Although Hillary (Rodham) Clinton is the first wife of a presidential candidate to have a career of her	Hillary Clinton's career was ignored by the media during her husband's campaign

own, media coverage of the 1992 presidential campaign focused more on her devotion to her husband and family, her appearance, and her personality than on her career. While some stories raised serious questions about her influence over the presidential candidate and about the possibility of an official role in a Clinton administration, many others were full of loaded language that conjured up negative images. While some stories addressed Hillary Clinton's views, others, many written by women presumably as career-oriented as their subject, addressed Hillary	for the American presidency.

Clinton's changing public image. Either these reporters didn't know how to write about this "new woman" in line to become the first lady, or it is simply the nature of the press to oversimplify." **-Pilloried Clinton,** *by Katherine Corcoran*	
"Universities, like cathedrals and parliaments, are a product of the Middle Ages. The Greeks and the Romans, strange as it may seem, had no universities in the sense in which the word has been used for the past seven or eight centuries. They had higher education, but the terms are not synonymous.	Early universities were not structured with classrooms but by close relationships with their educators.

Much of their instruction in law, rhetoric, and philosophy would be hard to surpass, but it was not organized into the form of permanent institutions of learning. A great teacher like Socrates gave no diplomas. If a modern student sat at his feet for three months, he would demand a certificate, something tangible and external to show for it— an excellent theme, by the way, for a Socratic dialogue. Only in the twelfth and thirteenth centuries do there emerge in the world those features of organized education with which we are most familiar, all that

machinery of instruction represented by faculties and colleges and courses of study, examinations and commencements and academic degrees. In all these matters, we are the heirs and successors, not of Athens and Alexandria, but of Paris and Bologna."
-The Rise of Universities, *by Charles Homer Haskins*

5. Answer the questions you find at the end of most textbook chapters! You can learn a lot by answering these questions, as they are often hints to the most important information you should have gathered from your reading.

Source Paragraph	Question
"You should not assume that your lecture notes are accurate and complete or that simply by taking notes you have learned the information the notes record. Two more steps are necessary: You must edit your notes, making them thorough and accurate, and you need to develop and use a system for study and review."	**What are the two most important steps after taking notes? Why are these the most important?** After taking notes, edit them for accuracy. Organize them, so they are easier to review later when you are studying the lesson.

-Study and Critical Thinking Skills in College, *K.T. McWhorter*	
"First, think about your audience. They are most important to the interpretation of your scientific message. However hard you try to send a clear message, the completed communication rests with them.	**Who is the audience of my writing? Why should I consider them?** You need to know your audience and who you are delivering your information to if you are going to write a message that is understandable to them.

> *You can't control an audience entirely, but since you are initiating the communication effort, you are responsible for presenting information in a way that is easily interpreted and understood."*
>
> **-Scientific Papers and Presentations,** M. Davis

Hour 9: How to Learn by Listening

Even with the best notes and reading skills in the world, some people will still always learn best by listening. These people are called auditory learners.

An auditory learner is someone that understands information best when they hear a lesson spoken or read aloud to them. These people flourish in settings were lectures are common. They are much different from their tactile learner counterparts because tactile learners are more hands-on. These are the individuals that do best when they are writing notes, reading, or trying new ideas out on their own.

If you consider yourself an auditory learner, it can be frustrating to think that the only success you will have in learning is through changing who you are. Fortunately, auditory studying is very successful as a method if done the correct way. Even for tactile learners, the ability to listen well can increase learning potential. There are a few steps that can be taken to ensure that you are doing everything you can to maximize your auditory learning.

1. **You should cancel out any other noises that might prove to be a distraction to you when you are focusing on an auditory lesson.**

As an auditory learner, sound will be the most important part of your learning experience. When listening to a recording, find a quiet place to do so where the noise from television, other people talking, or your roommate's music won't interfere. This method can also be very helpful with reading. Find a silent and private place and read your assigned text out loud to yourself. Hearing yourself as you read can be very helpful.

2. Some auditory learners consider hiring tutors to assist them in their learning.

Because it's easier to hear than read, a tutor can be helpful in note reviewing. They can read back through the information to you and help you understand key points you have missed. Hearing them speak the lesson to you might be easier than trying to sift through notated information and make sense of the lesson yourself.

3. Some Auditory learners also choose to record their lectures.

If you can, bring in an mp3 or tape recorder and document your lecture through recording. Most professors and teachers are more than happy to allow this if you ask. Be sure you sit at the front of the class where you will get a clear recording without interference. If you successfully record a lecture, you can listen to it over and over again in the weeks leading up to test day.

Remember how we discussed learning in your sleep in an earlier chapter? Recorded lectures are a great resource for that type of sleep studying.

4. **Toy with mnemonic games to remember important ideas.**

Turn information into song, rhyme or a word association game to get a better grip on it. Auditory learners have an easier time recognizing tunes and poems than they do with regurgitating written information. Young children are mostly auditory learners because they have yet to learn how to read or write. This is why nursery rhymes and songs are so important to them. The same method works throughout your life.

5. Whenever possible, seat yourself at the front of the class.

Many people dislike sitting at the front of the class because they feel it makes them more likely to be called upon or engaged with during a lecture. Speaking or answering difficult questions in public can be scary for many people. This is why the back seats of a classroom or lecture hall often fill up the fastest.

Auditory learners are doing themselves a disservice if they don't take advantage of open front row seats. From that vantage point, they can hear a clear and unobstructed lecture, which will help them better absorb what they are being told.

Hour 10: How to Cram before an Exam

If you find yourself in a situation where you have ignored all other information in this book and are suddenly faced with the need to cram for a test, there are a few things you can do to maximize your short-term learning.

First and foremost, give yourself a good stern warning that this information will likely not be long-term. Make a goal to practice better discipline in future study habits. Then, try out a few of these hints and tricks:

1. Get out of your usual living environment. You will have too many distractions at home. The television, your cell phone, and your computer will thwart your studying. If possible, leave them at home and go somewhere quiet where you won't be disturbed. Take your book, your notes,

and whatever bare necessities you will need.

2. Practice the 50/10 rule. This means you should study for fifty minutes, then take a ten-minute break. After ten minutes, return to your studying. Trying to study without breaks will only hurt you. Your mind needs time to clear between cramming sessions.

3. If you can handle it, study with a friend. Remind yourself not to get distracted and only work with a friend that you know will be helpful. Maybe your best friend is more fun to hang out with, but will they keep you focused on your studying or will you wind up going off topic and talking about other things? Make wise choices in study partners.

4. Focus on the big stuff. You probably don't need to know who discovered the atom so

much as you need to understand how atoms work and the parts of the atom that make it whole.

5. Break it into chunks if you can. Have you ever wondered why phone numbers are easier to remember than zip codes, despite being longer? It's because they are broken up into smaller sections.

6. Study out of order. You will get bored and overwhelmed if you read the same thing over and over again. Instead, find sections and mix them up, studying the parts you best understand first. Once you feel confident in a section, put it away and move onto something harder.

7. Sleep! The most important part of studying is making sure you get a good night's rest. Studies have been done to determine how well test-takers do when they have slept well and when they

haven't. Those who only studied a little, but got a full night's sleep did remarkably better in most circumstances than those who studied a lot and slept very little. Your brain won't function if it isn't rested.

Of course, cramming is not an ideal method and should never be relied upon. Always give yourself adequate time leading up to a test to study an appropriate amount of time each night. While the world can be a huge distraction, you shouldn't forget that learning is just as important as hanging out with friends. Sometimes, to be an efficient learner, you will need to prioritize your studies over a movie with your family or date night. In the short term, this is probably going to seem like a burden, but long term you will thank yourself.

Hour 11: Social Learning— Remembering Names, Faces, etc.

"I read in a book once that a rose by any other name would smell as sweet, but I've never been able to believe it. I don't believe a rose would be as nice if it was called a thistle or a skunk cabbage." – L. M. Montgomery

People's names are important. Getting a name wrong can be a huge hit to a person's self-esteem and relationships in general.

Have you ever had an awkward encounter with someone that seems to know and recognize you, but for the life of you, you can't name them?

This is a sticky situation to get out of and is best avoided. Some people, though, feel that they are just not able to remember faces and names. Is it true that some of us just aren't "wired" for social learning?

Absolutely not. For most who struggle in this regard, they just haven't learned the proper way to memorize other people.

By following the steps below, you can ensure that you are an apt social learner who will build better relationships with friends and co-workers and enhance your opportunities for networking throughout your life.

1. Make eye contact. Studies have shown that the eyes are the most instantly recognizable part of the face. If you take the time to learn someone's eyes, the rest of their face will be memorized more easily.

2. Repeat their name back to them. You don't have to be weird about it. Just

incorporate it into a greeting. For example, if you meet a new co-worker named Sharon, don't just say hello. Say, "Hi, Sharon. Nice to meet you." Saying a person's name helps your brain log that information for later use. Use their name throughout the conversation, but sparingly as not to appear strange. When you say goodbye, be sure to use their name one final time.

3. If the name is a unique one that you fear you won't remember, ask them for the spelling or for a business card. This will create a visual memory of the name that your brain can store away.

4. Find a way to associate their name with them, specifically. One suggestion is to use a rhyme. For example, if your friend introduces you to their friend, Brett, who served in the military, you might make a mental note of "Brett the vet." Alliterative

patterns can also help. "Nebraska Nick" could be another working example of this.

5. You can also make connections between people you meet and things you are already familiar with. For example, when meeting co-workers, you might have an easier time remembering a co-worker who has the same name as one of your parents. Look for ways to remind yourself of names as you are learning them.

6. The final way to ensure that you are learning names and faces properly is the simplest. Just make a decision to care. Most experts point out that memories are easier for us to hold onto if they are centered around things we think are important. You might be overwhelmed by the number of people you meet at a new job, but if you go into your first day with the attitude that all of these people will be

> important to you, it will be easier, in the long run, to associate their names and faces with their places in your life

The most important part of being a good social learner is finding balance in learning without appearing creepy or needy. When we spend too much time trying to learn about someone in a first encounter, it can come off as socially unacceptable. Maintain your composure and your manners, but do so in a way that helps you get to know the people you are now interacting with.

Soon, you will find that memorizing names and faces will come as second nature to you. Then, you will be able to relax and enjoy being a person that makes other people feel important. This quality is one that will get you far in career and social situations. You will make easier friends and build stronger professional relationships.

Hour 12: How to Become a Master Reader in Four Easy Steps

"You don't have to burn books to destroy a culture. Just get people to stop reading them." - *Ray Bradbury*

The best way to educate yourself is through reading. Literacy is, without a doubt, one of the greatest gifts our species has ever given itself. What do you do, though, if you feel like your ability to read and understand is subpar?

We all want to be readers. Here are a few steps you can take to ensure that you are reading to the best of your ability:

1. Read out loud. When people first learned to read, most didn't read in silence. Think about when you were a child. Most of the

reading you did was likely out loud to parents or teachers. This is because we learn our best when we hear the words as we read them. You might feel silly reading out loud by yourself (or to your pets), but once you get into a rhythm of it, you won't mind at all. You will actually be amazed at how much more you remember when you are finished reading out loud as opposed to what you are able to pick up during silent reading.

2. Think about a favorite film or song. Chances are, they moved you emotionally. You can likely remember quotes from your favorite movie or the lyrics to your favorite song because it is something that has importance to you on a personal level. You can use this same technique when you read. Even if you are reading a textbook, all you need to do is remind yourself that this book is part of an education and your overall plan for a

brighter future. As you read, keep in mind the relevance and the importance of the words. If you find a particularly interesting piece of text, take time to ponder it. Soon, you'll have a whole new appreciation for reading assignments.

3. Write what you read. Reading and writing go hand-in-hand when it comes to education and understanding. How you read will affect how and what you write. This is why the best writers in the world are usually some of the best readers, as well. Some people find that their best studying method is to write short essays about their latest reading, even if it is not an assigned task. When we write, we are forced to choose words that convey our understanding and how something has made us feel. We give ourselves a better understanding of subject matter by creating an opportunity to rehash it after it has been read.

4. Talk about what you have read. This works a lot like writing. When we commit ourselves to discussing our reading, we are forcing ourselves to check our own understanding. This is a crucial part of learning.

If you commit to using these steps in your reading and learning process, you will soon be a Master Reader. The process takes practice and commitment, but you will not fail unless you choose not to commit.

Remember, your educational future is in nobody's hands but your own. Make a wise choice to give yourself every opportunity that presents itself and make the most out of every chance you take.

Conclusion

Thanks for making it through to the end of *Accelerated Learning: Learn Faster and Improve your Memory Using the World's Most Advanced Techniques in 12 Hours or Less!* Let's hope it was informative and able to provide you with all of the tools you need to achieve your goals whatever they may be.

In a few weeks, feel free to retake the self-assessment found in Hour 2. You just might be amazed at how your study habits have improved!

The next step is to put what you have learned to good use. Maximize your potential as a student and lifelong learner. You will find that a whole world awaits you and that learning can be fun! The more you know, the better and more confident you will feel in any situation. You can advance your career, impress your friends, and better understand the things in this world you feel most passionate about, simply by allowing yourself to get excited about your education.

If there was ever a topic that interested you but seemed too complex, know that it isn't anymore. You are capable of understanding anything if you devote the time and the effort required to have a firm grasp of the related content. You set your own goals, and you determine your own horizons, so never sell yourself short!

Keep this book on hand if you ever need a reference point. Let it be the first of many books you add to your personal library of successes.

Finally, if you found this book useful in any way, a review on Amazon is always appreciated!

Made in the USA
Columbia, SC
22 November 2018